I0149681

RENOVATIO

RENOVATIO

bonafide rojas

Copyright © 2014 - Bonafide Rojas

All rights reserved. Except for brief passages quoted in newspaper, magazine, radio or television reviews, no part of this book may be reproduced in any form or by any means, electronic or mechanical, including photocopying or recording, or by information storage or retrieval system, without permission from the Publisher and/or Author.

Published in the United States by:
Grand Concourse Press

First Edition.

ISBN # 978-0615908175

Cover Design by:
VIKUBO

for my mother
my father
my sister
& my son

table of contents

introduction

I. *a long december*

II. *the missing words*

III. *strange days*

lament for a dying practice
the talking horse
the story of six
strange days indeed
mermaids in the canal
the cave
burning down the house

IV. *purple flowers*

home games
doo wop
revival to fly
the visits north
purple flowers
candles by the altar
the clean out
medicated slave
lefty
one year later

V. *just as the day was dawning*

the blind staggering drunk
sketches for my ex-sweetheart
the gambling highway
when in paris
the inevitable analysis...
just as the day was dawning

thank you's
biography

INTRODUCTION

what you are holding is renovatio, bonafide rojas'
third full-length collection of poems.

for those of us who have been avidly following
rojas' work since the '90s, the mere existence of
this to me is reason enough to celebrate.

rojas has always been a bard of the bronx, a new
nuyorican, a young poet committed to rebellion, in
love with great city. in his corpus, fool is a genius.
the block is byzantium. the id, innisfree. the
bronx, the body electric. the grand concourse, the
grecian urn. what yeats & keats saw in the
expanses of nature, the lore of antiquity, the objet
d'art rojas sees in his city & the souls that crowd
it, the teeming compendium of human sorrow
that is new york, every shattered window &
sagging train platform, every stoop & bier & all
they carry agony & unbounded love, scattered
cans & loose strands of lives.

& yet, something more is at work in this
collection. rojas may be the quintessential poet of
the nuyorican new wave, he may be our ginsberg
("holler" is our "howl"- i'll fight anyone who says
otherwise), yet here he becomes something greater
than these, he becomes himself. he settles into
stories like a man who has survived the inevitable
disasters. he eases his way around the brilliant
corners of his celebrated literary childhood into
what is unmistakably his seasoned adult voice.

he smuggles us to ease drop on "a conversation in a diner on the west side with someone who does not hear me speaking." he deftly references reed, dylan, marley, freewheels & free associates, yet is more fully in his body & the moment than ever. the constant musical motifs that pepper his work are no longer an escape from a harsh, unbearable world.

they are his companions in his commitment to the flesh, the carnal and fecund. even in the throes of a virtuosic romantic dismissal, he remains fully present, resists to urge to become overwrought, chides his would be lover to "cover the tip/make sure its decent."

the rojas we meet here is finely attuned to grit and detail ("the beauty of hard work/on my skin"), prescient ("he draws me again"), at times neruda-esque ("beautiful you are/in dawn, noon, dusk"), & at the same time, quintessentially rojas ("the poet in me/ hunkers in slim lighted tunnels/ searching for the nucleus of your howling heart").

he skips nimbly from haiku to pantoum to sonnet. he is less young hellion than sagacious craftsman, inverting symbols of his youth, scaling down the wild imagery of his earlier work. now, "the horses in our dreams/don't drag us apart anymore" & he admits, "i used to have a death wish/when i was younger but now/i want to be an old man."

the effect is work that is focused, lean, flayed of pity, but still rich with deep sentiment, flecked with hard earned lessons, redolent of the beauty & disaster that landed the poet here.

but when rojas drops "the old machine," it is clear our night has taken a turn. the work teeters deliciously between poetry & prose & reverberates with an eerie otherworldliness that is almost kafkaesque. it is allegory & infinitely personal. the reader may see in it an ode to a vanished new york, a rumination on age & death, & a pained paean to rojas' deceased father.

the metal may be both the sinister steel of developers & the nefarious needles of junkies. in "the old machine," father & son blend in a common grief. it is a brilliant work, utterly unlike anything rojas has written before, & links together an amazing web of influences, from bowie to borges.

when he recounts the great fire in "burning down the house," we see the new rojas, a man whose eyes are wild, but clear, whose entire life has erupted into flames, who has counted the cost, who has sifted the rubble, & has invited all of us over for gin & tonics. his smile is true & his hospitality sincere. he is a man who has survived the wringer & his tone is blood spattered & ferociously real.

he has already saved his most precious cargo "strange days," a love letter to his son is awash with child-like, beatlesque wonder & psychedelic merriment, & suffused with the heartache of fatherhood. he buries his own father with agonies of emotion, cursed by pitch-perfect recall and troubled by the clarity of reflection. in the end, he closes the casket with imperturbable calm.

the cycle of poems for his father "one year later," "home games," "doo wop," "revival," "the visits north," "purple flowers," "candles by the altar," & "lefty" are among the most beautiful & perfect poems he's ever written.

he closes by addressing his ex-sweethearts & asserting, for posterity, the wonders of peripatetic poesy, taking care to break our hearts along the way "i love you/& believe it so much, i sob after the echo" pressing a twenty into our palms & fixing us with a madman's smile before walking out the door.

"let the beauty of everything/be your beauty of everything/be the beauty of everything"

but never forget

"there's old man rojas, he's mad wild!"

the door clatters like a flapping jaw & he is in the night, boots clacking against the city's hide. everything is new again.

dennis kim/denizen kane
poet. emcee.
oakland, california
2014

RENOVATIO

THE LAST
EXTRAVAGANT MEAL

M O R N I N G (PT. I)

waking up before the sound of the alarm
always makes me weary about my patterns

i sit in silence & stare at the same ceiling
i've stared at for 30 years, i trace out the
cracks like i've done, a million times before

the time is 5:45am & i always wonder
can i function?

with less than 6 hours under my eyes
this bag of flesh is heavy with burden
for things i know & don't know

i am a very quiet man in the morning
i am routine, repetitive & reliable

i catch the same train
at the same time
monday through friday
& if i break routine i fear
i might walk into a stray bullet
only because i missed my
6:43 local train (so far i've been lucky)

i am sitting on bed
staring at the traffic lights
through the window

listening to the cars

& the people walking

smelling the beauty of hard work
on my skin & being grateful that today

i woke up again
& i'm promised
a few more hours
to love life.

A LONG DECEMBER

I.
when you left today
your stares felt like a tidal
wave of good bye knives

II.
your silence on the
phone is an echo that rips
right through my question

III.
i am the laughter
that my mother birthed after
her tears & heartbreak

IV.
the black in your eyes
is as bright at the first time
we made love that night

V.
the longing of your
touch is a memory that
i stroke myself with

VI.
son draws pictures of
us, his mother cuts me out
he draws me again

VII.
you are addiction
sweat broke you have made me whis-
per your name at night

VIII.
deconstructing kiss
bite lip, suck tongue, rip my face
off with your loving

IX.
even if your name
is tomorrow, i'll kill my
self not to see you

X.
love is a pistol
that you shoot blindly into
a crowd of hatred

XI.
unbreak the silence
that you slept with on nights you
should've said yes, please

XII.
this magic you are
is like alchemy, your breast
is an elixir

XIII.
i have paper where
my heart is, i draw colors
& hope you look in

XIV.
these moments are ours
no one can take them away
hold them close, real close

XV.
my father's quiet
with his love because he knows
i'm loud with my rage

XVI.
beautiful you are
in dawn, noon, dusk, your legs are
welcoming me in

XVII.
the hours of our
love are only counted by
the circles of sweat

XVIII.
the love i carry
is a knife i use to pro
tect me from self doubt

XIX.
i am still searching
for the right moment to tell
myself i love you

XX.
the flower you are
are the ones that all men want
defend your petals

XXI.
my snoring is act-
ually a love song that
you can't understand

XXII.
reinvent your love
for the machine you are is
imperfect like flesh

XXIII.
tonight is a re
minder that you'll still love me
even with my flaws

XXIV.
there are few things we
can do without damaging
ourselves, like loving

XXV.
how do your hands feel
after opening the door
you shouldn't have touched

XXVI.
in the black of night
i stare at the sky & pre
pare to eat the sun

XXVII.
in the eye of the
hurricane, i will stand in
it perfectly calm

XXVIII.
if you hold on to
pain, understand the torture
you carry with you.

XXIX.
leave the sun be, for
the ice & wind love me for
my heat & my eyes

XXX.
escape, is what we
need sometimes to totally
understand our love

U N : T I T L E D #1

i dream of finding you
in this cast of thousands

you're the one that stood out
in a room of friction & smoke

the magic potion you were carrying
was mythical, neither brain nor computer
can calculate how heavy you are

i'd have you still
even when time
is a broken thought
a feeling found in the seconds

stories born from fear
about a man who overcame
faults & flaws & learned

that hell is neither red nor chrome
but only carrying demons & doubt
there are ghosts born on the radio
on full moons & pitch black skies

with urges so real & so graceful
it becomes love ridden
i release this love that i have
worked for so long

& hope one day
it becomes a song.

THE SKELETON WOMAN

in this space of earth
there are objects, images, memories
strewn together with a thin strand of rope

a kneeling woman with her arms in the air
you sitting in blue with a flower in your hair
a photo of a hunter frightened by the prey
a pueblo that resembles warm comfort
olives, grape seed & apple vinegar
black kettles that hold your love
a fan brush of your laughter
four knobs on the oven
a mask framed in red
six blood oranges
a french press
abraxas

there's an army of ants following you
for they heard the dragonflies
say you were their queen
they heard the rumors from the bees
that you listen to them
they heard the stories of the spiders
that you will not kill them
until you ask them to leave

you will defend your home
with garlic & cinnamon

she can't save you
but she will help you save yourself

don't be wounded
when you approach her

just hold your flaws in one hand
& hope in the other

& she'll open the door for you
& you decide whether or not
you want to walk in.

SEARCHING FOR THE NUCLEUS OF YOUR HOWLING HEART

here
there is too much despair
& not enough of your smile

here
i make the best out of a moment
out of your wonderful scent
i can't erase you
i won't erase who you are

the poet in me
hunkers in slim lighted tunnels
searching for the nucleus
of your howling heart

your succulent mouth
the gin of a wednesday night
the tonic of a thursday morning

you are the one
i surrender my solitude for
crave your body heat to share my sheets

i love the way you are
magnanimous when you open
your hands & show me
a wonderful humble way of being

here
the poet in me is
delighted with your adventure

here
you are a witch
let us get high on your spells
radioactive & holy
we have magic in our body language

here
with you, it is not necessary to speak
the words i use here are not based on letters

here
let us sleep half bent
where no one will find us

here
when we awake, i'll write your name
on my skin & show it off like
the piece of art that it is.

KAMIKAZE LOVE DRESS

my lover's dress has always
been a sign of victory

my lover is not sweet
she's an atom bomb kisser

she is the river i drown in
she is the wind i throw cares into

she turns on the night with
her electric light laser beams

her garden is a love machine
something you never get used to losing

her love is the last living lilacs
of a glorious land of virtue & sin

she carries soaked rags
from a fountain of rain water

in the dark places
she's always wears white so i can see her

she breaks the branches of a day
to hang them on wires of tomorrow

on her forehead is the color
of her desire, not everyone can see it

her handwriting is scripted

31

for only women to read
she is ecstasies of good fortune
a place called home wearing
a kamikaze love dress

the wild in her dream rips her heart apart
she carry knives in her clutch
her name is a slow drug
that crawls off her tongue & up my spine

transfixed on the coming night
she stares into the whites
of my eyes, 3,000 miles away
so close yet so far

she is wearing the dress
for the next victory
& soaks it with the
blood of celebration

& i stand there with
a pocketknife
ready to run
all over this town

proclaiming my love for her.

MORNING (PT.II)

today i woke
up on my own
never set the alarm
not in a rush
i sit in silence
stare at the same
ceiling i've stared
at for 35 years
the only thing that
has changed are the walls
& the love laying
next to me, i've tried
to not keep the same patterns
the time is 11:17 am
& functioning is not
as important as happiness is
slept a full 8 hours
cleaned my bag
from unnecessary things
in the morning
i break routine
barely wearing clothes
listening the traffic
watching the sunlight
through my window
listening to the murmurs
of the street
stare at the beauty
of hard work
say goodbye to
the journals of my youth

i am grateful for today
i woke up again
& i'm promised
a few more hours to live
a few more hours to love.

THE LAST
EXTRAVAGANT MEAL

the last extravagant meal
has been eaten & i ended up with a red bowtie
the lady carries gingerbread in her mouth
today felt like the first day of spring

i ended up with a red bowtie
& spoke to my father 3 times
today felt like the first day of spring
& we laid in bed until it turned into evening

spoke to my father 3 times today
stared at the rubble of old yankee stadium
& we laid in bed until it turned into evening
saw my mother's mortality in her eyes

stared at the rubble of old yankee stadium
her skin smells like sugar
saw my mother's mortality in her eyes
she spoke with youthful optimism

her skin smells like sugar
it was a rather quiet day
she spoke with youthful optimism
she told me there was food on the stove

it was a rather quiet day
the lady carries gingerbread in her mouth
she told me there was food on the stove
the last extravagant meal has been eaten.

THE MAGICIAN

i didn't know you had magical powers
the kind that hover around you
like baby satellites but when you
walked away, i saw the universe

your hair as it played with gravity & waved
at me shaking stars out, crashing into the
concrete, the thing about stars in close
proximity is that they don't burn out
they stayed planted on the floor
like a trail for me to follow

you released wild animals from
your arms like parlor trick ponies
& polka dot zebras
it was so beautiful to watch

i was so mesmerized that at the very
next moment you disappeared like

a cloud of smoke
a flash of the hand
a fire in the sky
a bolt of blue lightning
tiny whirlwinds
a pair of crashing mirrors
& no one saw it
to give you
a standing ovation.

CONVERSATION IN A DINER ON THE WEST SIDE WITH SOMEONE WHO DOESNT HEAR ME SPEAKING

it's alright, you know
this will allow me
not to carry the weight
i normally would

the ballads that expand in my head
are endless but i try not to think too
much & hope everything turns
out for the better

the winds are intense today
i'm going be a lonely man
when you go

but before you do
meet me in the morning
at our favorite spot on broadway & 175th st
to eat our favorite meal
eggs benedict for you, steak for me
lets make it nice & simple

this is the fifth time around
& i still get visions of you
dressed in baby blue

walking on the west side

where the walls are high
& its easy to laugh & hard to cry
just one more cup of coffee
even though i will only order gin
yes, this early

would you like to come over?
i understand if you don't
i'm a what?

oh, you have to go?
no, we can stay here all night
they wouldn't kick us out
you have a bottomless cup

it's alright, i just wanted you to know
you're still on my mind, its been non-stop
i was hoping for a i'll be your baby kind
of night, to be alone in a dream kind of day
but i know its a i threw it all away
type of situation

but is one more night
that too much to ask
tell me if you don't want that
yes i know what you said before
i was hoping for a different answer

when i get trouble of the body or
sorrow of the spirit, i think of calling you
i sometimes can be a man of tomorrow
but not today, today is celebration
of this wonderful meal, right?

can i have a glass of water please?
no more gin today, if you have
to go i understand

i'll get the check
you cover the tip
make sure its decent

we've been here too long
bottomless cups end eventually

let me get the door for you
which way are you going?

me?
i'm going north
oh, your going south

ok, maybe i'll see you
on the west side sometime

i'll look for baby blue.

THE MISSING WORDS

SUNDAY AFTERNOON REALIZATION OF IMPERMANENCE

today is another day i will collect
full of light, clouds, sky & sounds
the concrete is welcoming

there is a beautiful calmness
in the day, that as chaotic
as it can be opened itself to me

what i know is but a microcosm
of what i will eventually know
this moment is but a breath
of what i'll gather in my life

everyday i feel my mortality
a twitch in body
an ache in bones
the shortness of breath that
wasn't there before

last night was another that i collected
one that has layers of skin & whispers
that will resurrect themselves in the future
as oxygen, wind & memories
& i will put them in a box until that day

i will watch the dust dance into
a song of life, one that i can sing
the melody & i can eat the words

i used to have a death wish
when i was younger but now
i want to be an old man

one that appreciates
the beauty of counting wrinkles
& opening boxes.

SONNET #7

you decode my language
because you think there might be something
that you'll find that will save you
like a stampede of bricks falling from my
mouth, you take cover from the words i create
(because after creation will come action, then
reaction) & you've taught me not to react

but to accept this tongue that chokes
my throat with contradictions
& compliments, we make an oath to be quiet
to absorb music & bathe each other
& when the red lights are on
we appreciate patience like bread
& make love on holy glitter.

THE OLD MACHINE

the old man nervously walked back to his
apartment. tonight was fun, but during this
midnight arrival he noticed the missing hand
on his left that morning he said nothing while
drinking gin & tonics. he put a metallic
replacement on his wrist.

he looks into the mirror & asks himself,
"see what you did now, what's going to
happen next?" he shakes his head, turns the
lights off & walks out the room

the next morning the sun rose very slow
slower than usual. when the old man woke,
his metallic hand extended to his whole arm
his right foot was also missing, he didn't know
why

he thought about the week before & what he
ate: chicken, red meat, pasta, aluminum, pizza,
salad, rice & beans, & he realized maybe the
amount of aluminum has something to do
with the growth of his metallic hand

later that morning he attached a metallic foot.
he understood that his obsession with
aluminum is affecting his metallic organ
growth but all of a sudden he has gotten a
burst of energy.

weeks later half of the body of the old man

is aluminum but he feels thirty years younger
he used to dream about the beauty of robots
now he wakes up energized, electric,
mechanic, but not a man anymore, not a full
man, his veins are wires, his heart still
pumping, his bones are a mixture of nuts,
bolts & cartilages.

every morning the old machine nervously
walks back to his apt & this time he noticed
he had to plug himself in the socket his
battery is running low & he has work the do.

II.

the old machine remembers when he was fully
organic, made of flesh, blood & bones, young
& vibrant but growing up in the inner city was
hard when it came to meals you had to eat
whatever you could get your hands on

one summer everything was scarce except for
aluminum. at first, he was hesitant to eat it but
was told it would do nothing to him. when
you're hungry, you're hungry, so he started
eating everything so often & never assumed
anything would be wrong

while other kids in the neighborhood ate
copper & brass, he stayed with aluminum, got
laughed at by the suburban kids who ate silver
& platinum, only the very well off ate gold
but he heard it could become very addicting

to eat the rich metals, now in his old age he's
finally witnessing the effects of his odd diet.
he called doctors, engineers &carpenters &
asked if they ever heard of what was
happening to him, they all said no. he called
his childhood friends & the ones alive said
they stopped eating metal decades ago

so here's the old machine, confused about the
situation staring in the mirror every morning
& seeing the aluminum crawl inch by inch &
all he can do is try to control his appetite &
try not to get magnets stuck on him

III.

yesterday his battery finally gave out, he had
his doctor recommend a mechanic that would
sell him the parts he needs no one likes to be
jump started in the street

his rotator cuff needs more oil, his joints are
rusting up, the old machine used to dream
about death & what happens afterwards, how
the light or darkness

comes to greet you, but nowadays he thinks
he'll end up in the scrap yard with all the
other machines, they can gather around, play
cards, bingo & talk about the good ol days

when they were young men running around
with two fresh feet, flesh footed running on

the beach "do you remember the good old
days" they asked the old machine he replied
with a stark stare & slow drawl

yes, yes i remember the non rickety days
where all i would want was to prevent myself
from getting cut but these days being cut &
seeing blood would be the most magnificent
thing, to bite my fingernails off, to spit saliva,
to comb my hair, to wear prescription glasses
those things made me so human, those things
i miss the most.

IV.

i remember i used to run across the fields as a
child, wonderfully green & sky blue so
beautiful it used to make me cry

but now these eyes of mine are dim the
vibrancy is fading, i need to put small light
bulbs in place so people know i am still alive,
my smile is steel frame

the aluminum has covered ninety percent of
my body, only my head remains flesh from my
neck down, i am a glorious silver, when i
touch my chest i do not feel a heartbeat

i feel a small engine revving up but there
is no a revolution in me, i am compromised
i have assimilated into the twenty first century
as a boy i had dreams of androids & robots

but this is no dream, i feel my brain getting
closer to failing & being replaced by a
processor so i can become live once again, but
i do not want to be reincarnated into a newer
machine

i have lived decades with these flaws of man
with these character traits of insecurity with
these prejudices that i learned from my father
with this face from the old country

i am a documentation of my family, a living
memory, a breathing conversation, why has
this happened to me? was this put in motion
the minute i ate my first piece of aluminum?
why won't my flesh fight back for survival?
where are my white blood cells? can't they see
they are being colonized?

at night when i sleep my body becomes so
cold, my gears need oiling every morning,
i dont know who i am anymore

the internal battle i have of "man vs machine"
is not an overstatement, i can feel my organics
becoming metallicity, my mechanic calls it
metallogenic (i have no clue i'm an old man)

the other night i walked into the wall
because my sight gave out and when i came
too, i was bleeding black oil from my mouth
where is my blood? what have i become? if i
sleep will i awake a new machine? will i retain

my memories? am i dying? is this what death
is? losing control of your body, having
something control it without my permission.

V.

in this kingdom of flesh
my bones were brittle & worn
& i've come to terms with the fact
i am not as young as i used to be

while others push their flesh back
to maintain their appearance
i've waxed this silver to sparkle & parade

i replaced my hair
with different colored fedoras
& my eyes look like marbles
but are far from it

i'll never see the proud chalk
of my bones wear down with age
i have a six cylinder inside of me

no more carrying wrinkled paper faces
& ink stained smiles
my battle scarred galactic badges
of survival are ones i show off
& tell people stories about
look at this imperfect machine of man
where he will break, rip, tear, bleed & bloat
i am nothing like that
people laugh as the badges fall off

because they cannot be pinned
i search for magnets

i did want my son to see my skin
to wonder what is being held
in these bags of stories

but no more

i warn him not to mimic the reflections
of moving pictures, that they mimic parallel
universes of being disconnected & flawless
all things we shouldn't be in life

they have been built on stage lights & green
screens, we are not fiction or fantasy
but documentations of a continuing
experience

he calls me hypocrite, full of "aluminum &
regret"

i told him i was once the youngest man in the
room, hyper, energetic, hurricane like
they spoke of me like:

"there's rojas, he's mad wild"

carrying a death wish to die young
like a match burning rapidly
but all that changed when you were born
i wanted to watch you grow

i wanted to be the old man storyteller
but you'll would never see him
we'll always ponder the "what if?"

my motor skills are steady
sometimes my gyroscope needs adjusting

i long for the days to smell bread
inhale steam from the pots
stare at the ocean for hours
with no fear of rust

i don't stop to smell the roses anymore,
i can't enjoy art either,
i'm color blind now
wisdom is not for the young
the youth cradle spontaneity
& curiosity i tell him
"don't eat metal, regardless how good it
tastes"

i used to be the youngest man in the room
& always felt honored to be allowed in
"don't ever forget your place, son, you might
have people waiting for you"

i told him i want people to speak of me in my
old age like:

> *"there's old man rojas, he's mad wild!"*

WHEN THE VOICE IS SILENT

there are days
i have nothing to say
only the thoughts exist

my voice is non-existent
the body lays silent
the broken clock stays on a second
the sirens from the street
sound like armageddon

i want to cover myself from
the world but really from you

there are days that i find you
in a different body
find you in a place where i
extremely don't want to be

where the lights are gloomy
& the nights is neon
that produce a vibration
i keep in my skull to never speak

nights that being in a room full
of people make me want to vomit
there are days i write
because there is no other option.

NOTE TO SELF TO PUT ON THE REFRIGERATOR

remember to
pace yourself
breathe
know that this
is not the end
ramble less
think more
smile even more
learn your heart
unlearn your aggression
be more optimistic
be less pessimistic
understand that this
is easier said than done
say a prayer
once in a blue
& don't even
call it a prayer
call it talking
to yourself like
it actually is
its good to hear
yourself talk sometimes
wake up &
say thank you
for another day
cook your own meals
even the bad ones
feed your soul

drink less soda
yes i said less soda
i am obviously
talking to myself here
today i have drank no soda
only juices & water
lets hope this routine sticks
love your body
you only have
one at a time
when your back hurts
rest
when your legs hurt
rest
when your eyes hurt
rest
i am telling myself to
rest
i hope you read this often
tell your son
you love him dearly
tell him so much
it annoys him
one day he'll thank you
tell your mother
you love her
because she annoys you
& know you
will miss her immensely
when it's her time
but for now
she's a spark plug
love your art

& you art will love you back
love your pain
it will heal everything
love your friends
because they are patient with you
love your enemies
because they are potential friends
stop being a sarcastic asshole
stop being stand-offish
stop being a know-it-all
stop being a thief
stop being a liar
stop being everything
you learned when
you were a boy
that you felt
protected you from
things that scared you
you're an adult now
which really means
you have more bills
now only be scared
of what you don't try
be scared of what
could have been
be scared that
this version of yourself
could be better
if you dropped all
the bullshit
you carried in life
it weighs your arms down
then you'll have

no time to do
the beautiful things
you love to do
like write
play guitar
pick up your son
pour yourself a gin & tonic
on your day off
eat pizza
have a glass of sangria
from camaradas el barrio
look for new blazers
get some new shoes
some things are
worth being routine
others should be slightly erased
so you can see the lines
but not the whole action
be grateful
& say thank you
when it is needed
it will bring out a smile
& smiles are beautiful
remember to be patient
& pace yourself.

M O R N I N G (PT. I I I)

in this morning of wonderful silence
i stare at the small piece of wonder you are

how your breath room rotates
around the sunlight
i count the raindrops on the window
the wood panels
the steps of the wolf
running in your stomach

let us stretch our limbs across
this room that has not let go of night

let us dream in a second
& see the day pass us by

here we communicate through body & stare
no volume of voice is allowed
hand gestures & hip movements only

when i raise myself from the earth
i dust myself off & offer you
yesterday's shredded skin as a present

MEDITATIONS IN L'ENFANT PLAZA

in the midst of this city's noise
i search for the reason
in the quiet of my anger

i listen to my breath expand my sternum
straining to keep everything in place

observe the sun fight through the clouds
i notice it's everlasting struggle

i filter decisions
through a funnel of clarity & experience
this is not the same moment
i've lived a decade ago

with each minute i change intrinsically
& extrinsically change like suns, skies
& oceans

they look like they haven't changed
but are always evolving

in the noise of my bones
in the outskirts of my islands

i am searching for the reasons & the answers
to the questions i haven't asked yet.

THE MISSING WORDS

i have spent hours on
each side of the continent
searching for the missing words
that belong in my sentence

i have written & ripped apart line after line
looking for a moment captured indelibly

i have seen the sun rise in brooklyn
& set in san francisco
counted stars in the aurora of miami
& watched the black accept the sun in paris

i am a lucky man
i repeat that phrase as a reminder
to keep my feet still

i have taunted & been taunted
i have broken & been broken
i have eaten & have fed
i have lied to myself & spoken honestly
& they both have hurt me
i complicate & simplify

there are wonderful times when i am very
confused & there are horrendous times
when i am very logical

who knows my voice when i am silent?
how does my touch feel when i have cut
my hands off?

your watchful eyes keep memory in print
your mind knows not the tricks it plays on you

i have spent days walking streets
with the same name in different cities
looking for an answer in the intersections

i stand on the corners
comfortable in my skin
as i always hope to be
the longer i can stand upright
have hands that work & legs that move
i spend time searching
for a tomorrow that will show me
something beautiful

the past is chaptered
barely remembered
but has become legacy
through documentation

i am a lucky man
there were times when the road was so dark
i just stood there, too scared to move
then when the sun rose, it allowed me
to walk in daylight, literally

i've seen stray bullets puncture friends
& the walls of my home

i've seen people's face
ripped off in a crowd
of celebration

people i loved have
taken their own lives
that could of have been
me in every case
but i was always fearful
of not seeing what could be
the great unknown
is not death but tomorrow
i want to see
the repercussions
& celebrations that
come from my decisions

i am still searching for
the missing words
in my sentence

i am a lucky man.

UN:TITLED #11

immortality accepts
no expectations
romance only knows
three words

& the lengths
we would go for both
depend on our feet
are they willing to walk
the miles unknown

this modern world
of relationships
doesn't allow me
to love you at first sight

there are no princesses
in distress anymore
we figured out that the
concept of princesses
in distress were made up
by men anyways

the princes have
changed their names to
protect their legacies
against leeching family
members & lustful scorpions
with lipstick on

we're taught not to dream anymore

our childhood ghosts
have remained trapped
in the back cabinet
of the closet
they hold our imagination
like a blanket

our little brothers
believe in the motion pictures
of guns & drugs on the television

they emulate the concrete
in front of them
& became the hard rocks
we can't break through

our little sisters grow up too fast
to notice that they were wearing
their older sisters skin

there was no need for them
to stay young because
the generation before them were
having too much fun

the black steel was taken off
the windows & let in the guilty
pleasures of the world

like the sugar they indulged
too much of & now all their teeth
are rotten

only love can heal their heart
open their sarcasm
to the hope of being healed

do not wait 400 years
to save generations
of children who lost
their innocence because
their parents were to busy
working to keep us alive
feed them the passion of survival

immortality accepts
no expectations

romance only
knows three words

but are they
beautiful or hateful?

THE NEED OF BEING VERSED IN CITY THINGS

the building needs repairs again
the super's name is persio
a dominican man that loves
bruce springsteen, he's a good man

the elevator breaks down often
walks up in this city feel like your climbing
a mountain, count the steps, i bet you you'll
stop at a hundred

from my window you can see the bedrooms
across the street, i try not to look too often
but a naked woman will always distract me
from the stars

listen to the cars talk to each other
through engine, through screech,
through beat, through horn,
they have an odd language

respect the concrete for holding itself
together even when the trees try to
break through with their roots
trying to reclaim what's theirs

learn to read the subway map
as if you've seen it before
be weary of shady characters
when asking for directions

always ask different people
never carry a map in the street
it looks like a cape, never listen to manuals
or tourist guides when it comes to food in
this great city, ask the people coming out
ask the people who work next door

they will tell you the truth
no grades or no celebrity chef
no shiny lights or visits from diplomats
ask the workers

when you're walking the street
observe the people who you think
are from the city, look at their steps
their speed, follow them,
don't be a slow walker

this city is beautiful & we know
you want to see every inch of it but
for the sake of not putting yourself in danger

do not be a slow walker!

there are many things people from
this city will disagree on: their sports teams,
where the best pizza is or when is the best
time to visit but they'll all agree you'll never
leave after you get here.

REMINDERS OF LUCK

today will be the first day
that i have accepted that
i have only started to love
myself, that everyday before this
was just survival & i never
gave myself enough time
faith to tell myself the things
i needed to hear & to accept
everyday is a reminder of
how i am alive & beautiful
but i only believe half of it
on a day where the memory
of my friend louis lingers on paper
a man named jack says goodbye
& a woman named lucille told me
to celebrate with her, i am moved
to tears that i am lucky enough
deserving enough to take another
breath, to have another day to explore
the inside of me, to make me acceptable
to me, that i am lucky enough to sit here
& speak to my son & share secrets with him
call my mother & tell her i love her, of course
i fall in the same cycles & traps we all do
based on things we can let go but tomorrow,
that wonderful day of tomorrow, will teach
me how to let go & stop worrying & accept
the reminders of my day & whisper them into
my skin. i love you.

(& believe it so much, i sob after the echo).

STRANGE DAYS

D E A R E S T

dearest
i am still standing here
holding our past like a broken vase
the water has damaged
my good pants it's okay
they're only pants

are my pants a metaphor?

there's nothing in the vase
only cracked pieces of glass
that have cut into my hand
the blood has stained my shirt sleeve

is my shirt a metaphor?

my feet are straining to stand
it's been days, i'm impressed
i haven't collapsed

with every day that passes
i wonder will you return
i didn't mean to break the vase

        is the vase a metaphor?

or my tired feet?

everything has dried up
my pants are still damaged
my shirt is still stained

i have scars on my hands
my feet are bruised
i am still standing here

the vase
i threw it out finally

my hands grew tired
of holding the past

are you a metaphor?

or am i?

OCEANIC

these oceans
we carry are massive

we are tidal waves
waiting to burst

crashing against
the edges of our skin

the sand in our mouth
is a reminder of the water

we are

these bodies we float in
are enormous

we get lost

shipwrecked during our travels
we never carry compasses

we search for the secluded land
of our hearts

the uncharted islands
of our ribs

let us discover peninsulas
in our legs

archipelagos
in our stomachs

let us discover
the mariana trench

of our voices,
dangerous, beautiful

this journey will last
as long as our langers

let us find
the new land of our lives.

ANAGRAMMABLE

(instructions: after reading each word take a breath)

(alive)

a

live

(breakdown)

break

down

(hopeful)

hope

full

(searching)

search

in

(heart)

hear

art

(inside)

in

side

(everybody)

every

body

(belonging)

be

longing

(supernatural)

super

natural

(flower)

flow

lower

(beautiful)

beauty

full

(forget)

for

get

(forgive)

for

give

(healing)

heal

in.

LAMENT FOR A DYING PRACTICE

twenty years ago
i would rewind my favorite song
over & over until it was
burned in my psyche
& i could recite the lyrics verbatim

the worst thing that could
happen is the radio would
eat my cassette & i would
pull it out with its guts
stuck to the teeth of the player

the first life saving act i would
do is rewind the cassette
& pull the tape back inside
with the hope of salvation

when done, press play
cross my fingers & listen

i was okay with a small part
of the song being distorted
as long as it wasn't in the climax
of the song, this time the tape
in question it didn't survive
these were the ways of old

fifteen years ago
i carried compact discs

that were compiled by hours
of pondering which album
i would want to carry with me
a small case full of melody
& emotional attachment to every artist
who could fit comfortably
in my backpack or jacket pocket

i would carry the twelve cd's
sometimes only for one song
but it was worth it, pressing the button
for the automatic replay
would free my hands to do whatever
was intended for them

when a cd would get
scratched, i would do everything in my
power to fix it, to this day
once i have a scratch, i have tried
the hundreds of methods
but none really ever work

after i received my first computer
i quickly learned the joy of playlisting
& burning cd's, i felt like the greatest dj
in the world, gone were tapes made for
pretty ladies now i made cd's for them
& if i liked a girl enough
i would show my depth in the choices

remember making a mixtape/cd
is important, if she doesn't like it
you're done, music taste is a part

of the decision process

i have so many blank discs
with random words on it
specifying when & where
the disc was made & i would listen
& be unsatisfied with the selections
but its okay, this is a learning process
same thing happened with cassettes

once to memorize a song, i recorded it
over & over again on a 60 minute tape
i will not reveal the song for the sake of
maintaining respect

but now this practice is almost gone
i speak to purists & traditionalists
about purchasing their favorite tape/cd

the white album double cassettes
the infamous purple tape
the hendrix box set i brought in paris
the original fondle 'em vinyl i still own

i reintroduce myself to a past time
that is cemented in my youth of
pause, stop, record, & play
& it is immortal.

THE TALKING HORSE

the golden hanoverians
are discussing about talking equines
"if god exists then god is a black stallion"

the american saddle horses says nothing
but exhales fire & rage
they're obnoxious but usually
have the bee stung tongues

the shetlands say nothing
so no one says anything to them anyway

the dartmoor ponies are rioting
saying "we've been lied to, look at us!"

the burning palominos are always
rambling & the andalusians
always ignore them
they've always thought of
themselves as spaniards
(instead of actual horses)

when the zebras want to
say something
they are cut off by the
other horses don't
listen to them, they're
considered mutts, mullatos,
african stripes & they respond
"but we're horses first!"

the golden hanoverians
are discussing about talking equines

"if god exists then god is a black stallion"

the golden hanoverians said
"all of you would of realized it
but you were busy with
your heads up your asses
running in movies like seabiscuit
or making commercials like those
stupid clydesdales that
work for budweiser

the clydesdales shouted in defense
"come on, we're just working give us a break"

the appaloosa whispered
"they're sell outs"

the onlookers were amazed
because they never knew
horses knew how to speak english
let alone argue with each other &
have discussions about god.

THE STORY OF SIX

you have such a strange reputation
don't you six
if you're with your brothers
you become the a trio of evil incarnate
why? because someone crazy said so
why would anyone believe crazy people
why didn't they ask you?
isn't reputation an odd thing
if five & seven didn't like you
they would make you nine
how would eight feel about this?

all it ever takes is a group
of people to damage a reputation
you should gather some threes
& a few plus signs & start your own
defense committee

why not if 9 was 6? why not 999?
why are you the only single number with an x
like a bullseye, maybe you should
reinvent yourself to "si. x"
say your puerto rican & call yourself: "yes ten"

yes!

confuse people & call yourself "xis"
they won't even know the difference
but you'll need to start a new campaign
like "why six & not si. x"
it will work great in latin america

you will need a publicist & an agent
a manager for talk shows
& prepare a strong defense

be careful with republicans
they'll say you're being un-american
even though numbers & english
are not an american concept
be careful with assimilation
trademark this move
star yourself in the movie
make a cameo on oprah
write a biography called "3+3 = me"
live in hollywood
hang out in soho
date models who are thinner than you
but remember where you came from
in between 5 & 7, don't think you're
the only number out there
i've seen it happen with 1
everyone used to say "one"
& 1 thought, i don't need anyone anymore
until deuces came out
remember how fickle people can be
don't be a story on page six in the paper
always remember, who was with
you in the beginning
you've always been my favorite

si. x
welcome to the new world.

MERMAIDS IN THE CANAL

on verversstraat centrum
i can see mermaids in the canals pushing
together the leaves to make a blanket
they hitch rides on water taxis
never pay fares & flick off the drivers
they are a wild bunch

they speak a mix of dutch & surinamese
they wrote it on a piece of paper for me
called it durinamese

they're parents came from suriname
after the december killings
many of their mothers were from
paramaribo, great great grandparents
were tainos & africans
they said they could hear
the bronx & boriquen in my accent

they all have a red stripe on the their
back with a yellow star in the middle to
symbolize their love for suriname

they asked me for chocolate, followed
me down the canal, asked to touch my
hair since mine was dry & theirs rarely
ever was, they are beautiful brown with
features ranging from indonesian to
dutch to middle eastern

at any given moment
one of the mermaids would whisper
justitia : pietas : fides
one after another
justice : duty : loyalty
a surinamese motto

i asked them why didn't they go
back to suriname
& they spoke of the president
dési bouterse & how he killed
& enslaved their family
to dig for gold at the bottom
of the ocean

so they came here
some traded their fins for legs
to blend in, to assimilate
to be free of the burden
of being a mermaid

but not them
they loved the water too much,
they speak of having no boundaries
visiting wherever they want
spoke about the community they have
& how they feel responsible
to keep this memory alive

that they existed peacefully
they were many before
they don't want to be exotic
they only want to swim & laugh

i asked about the leaves
they were collecting
they told me in the winter
they sleep in leaf based cocoons
at the bottom of the canal
to keep them safe & warm

i told them i will be back here
in the spring with chocolate
waiting for their first swim
saying hello to them in durinamese.

STRANGE DAYS
INDEED

these are strange days
aren't they john pablo?

the other day, we saw elephants
running down the west side highway
with ties & hats on, saw a pack of tigers
sunbathing in brooklyn bridge park
one even jumped in the river

saw some mimes at a concert
but the band looked sad
because there weren't noisy responses
at the end of the songs

we saw lightning dance over
the atlantic ocean, i don't think
they knew we were watching them

saw pigeons play baseball in yankee stadium
we were peeking from the train platform
one even slide home

we saw gorillas in guerillas suits on
dancing with republicans while
the democrats sang them love songs

these are strange days
aren't they john pablo?

the other day, we saw hypocrite liars
tell us the honest truth about how they
felt about me, it wasn't all good but honest
nonetheless

saw dancers stand in a row
protesting the lack of originality
in the music that was being released

we saw a cloud play some songs
in a key we never heard of
in a tune that we didn't know
but it still sounded like the beatles

saw water dancing in the sun
not worried about drying away, it said
"its cool baby, we always come back down"

we saw eyes on every building corner
winking at us when we walked by
i think they saw something they liked

saw flowers bloom in winter
a beautiful blue smelled like a mix
of lavender & oakland

we saw people love each other
purely. simply. beautifully. wonderfully
it was a spectacular sight

these are strange days
aren't they john pablo?
"most peculiar" he said.

THE CAVE

there are no caves
in my chest anymore
everything has been
exploding & paved
for streets & buildings
for the progression
of the society of my bones

there are no caves
on these fields for
me to run from all
the worries & fears
that have hung
in my skies like kites
eclipsing the sun

there are skyscrapers
on my ribs puncturing
my esophagus
when i breathe i swallow
glass & brick
there is no easy way
to accept my life
has been built
without my approval

there are no caves
but highways above my heart
driving past never stopping
to see the beat that pumps
to see the blood that's beautiful

to see the music of each second
i'm even too busy
to see the pollution
the highways are causing
too busy to notice
there's no skyline anymore
because someone has built
banners across my sky

i want to the see the beautiful flesh
of my stomach stretched out to see
the colors of the universe i hold inside

there are no caves here
no place for me to hide or keep things secret
no place for me to be young again
or to die old gracefully

there are bridges on my sternum
connecting the ever growing
illusion that this life is the only
one i've ever had, but these trees
that are now gone, were planted
by me once before, when the sun was
only blocked by the clouds of my sorrow

there is a myth on my wrists
that i was established 36 years ago
but these feet have walked a million miles
beyond my imagination
these hands have touched a million things
beyond my comprehension
like love

love is & will always be beyond
my comprehension
that's why every part of me
is still searching for it

& let the love i find
reign on me like a natural force
of the universe that it is

there are no caves left except for one
beneath my right muscle
where everyone forgets to check
because its bothersome
that's where i keep all the
things i hold sacred

& if i ever allow you in
you'll see drawings of me by my son
then you'll see me

beautiful like my son sees me
beautiful like my son sees me
beautiful like my son sees me

that's what i keep safe.

BURNING DOWN THE HOUSE

if my house ever burns down
i know i'll only have two minutes
to choose exactly what needs to be saved
& what i can remember
if it's lost in the fire

i'll have to concentrate
even with the sensation
of five hundred degrees in my face
full of smoke, sweat in my eyes,
i'll have to concentrate & decide

first things first
think of all the important things in my life
the photos that can't be recreated
the paintings of dead family members
the winnie the pooh doll that reminds me
of my son as a baby

then the things i've worked so hard for
the guitars, the amps, the dreams,
the hopes, the hours, the dedication,
the childhood & then there's the poems
i have to save the poems even the ones
i despise, they have to be saved
they saved me so i have to return the favor

then its the books, the small collection
that turned into a small library

i have to save some of those

the first edition neruda's & garcia marquez's
the signed baraka's & the junot diaz with the
geeky joke he wrote to me

the five most important poetry collections
that makes breathing possible, the painting
that stands in my living room has to be saved,
i've let all the other paintings die
except that one

the only framed photo
of my mother & father
the one with them smiling
still married, on vacation
both still young, still active

the red acoustic that has been
in my possession longer than
anything else, survived
the pawn shop runs
when i sold my first stratocasters
survived both apartments in chicago
scratches & dents a plenty, a broken head
stock, a raised fret, only wearing
four strings, remember to take that
dust her off & play an a chord

its been a minute & a half
almost everything has been
thrown out the window
hopefully everything survives

the clothes will burn quickly
the magazines will light instantly

then grab a few dvd's, the special ones
like star wars, the beatles set, def poetry
i forgot fight club but i think it would have
wanted it that way

the last things i grabbed were my briefcase
boxes, i tripped over the hard metal shell
half burned, i almost forgot it & have
a bruise from the fall

i couldn't take my door that has
twenty years of sticker collecting
my hendrix posters or my radiohead vinyl
many things had to be left

but there are some things
that are meant to go up in flames
for a reminder in the sky

so that when i look up
the smoke will linger
especially the ones that
have music in them.

PURPLE FLOWERS

HOME GAMES

there are a few things in life
my father & i enjoyed together
a plate of rice & beans
acting a fool for family
& baseball

all of the fond memories
i have of my father are either
in yankee stadium or watching a game

i once asked him who his favorite player
was growing up, i remember him saying
clemente but i don't recall any of other names

we shared the yankees like bread,
compared stats, a distaste for the mets
but he appreciated them because they had
so many latinos at the time

we went to a lot of games
& one of the last things
my father ever brought me
was the memorial patch
for the old stadium
as if he knew a part of us was gone

in the year before he died
he called me occasionally
asking if i wanted to catch a game
with him but i always
pretended to be busy

& we never caught that game
he wanted to go to

so the day after his funeral
i went to a game realizing
we would never share this experience again

i stood on the upper decks
watching the stadium empty out
& i cried

because even though we never truly
understood each other
we always used baseball as a metaphor

we would bunt our conversations along
hoping to get one of us home.

D O O W O P

on the rare nights
when i would visit my father

he would be listening to his favorite groups
the platters, the stylistics & the four tops
doo wop

he grew up in the bronx in the 60's
but i never understood
why he didn't fully embrace rock&roll
like i probably would have

he said "i like the beatles early stuff
then everything got louder & weirder, plus
i still had doo wop & salsa & you couldn't
dance to rock&roll."

i know what he meant
there's no slow dancing in pink floyd music
just slow music

you can't play led zeppelin
in a house party hoping to catch
a girl's eye during a john bonham drum solo

i raised myself on rock & roll & stayed away
from salsa, it never connected to it the way my
parents did but when i discovered the fania
all-stars, now i understood & appreciated it
so much more like we connected for second

every now & then
i'll play some doo wop
light a joint like my father would

listen to these
4 or 5 man groups harmonize
pretend i'm in the harlem
or the south bronx
of my parent's memory

& see him standing there
snapping his fingers
keeping the beat.

REVIVAL TO FLY

maybe one day
you'll see the world
through the eyes
of a reincarnated bird

i only say a bird
because you've been
grounded for so long
the next time around
maybe all you'll want to do is
see things from a higher perspective

go south for the winter
have something to call your own
start a new family
teach your children how to fly
build a nest in joyce kilmer park
by the bronx supreme court

& when you see your friends
from the old neighborhood
who have been reincarnated too
all of you can call each other jail birds
laugh & just fly away.

THE VISITS NORTH

the bus rides at 5:00 am
to visit my father in jail
when you're 9 years old with
a grandmother you barely speak
to might as well be a mission to mars
& i was an untrained astronaut

what i remember from those trips
are the street lights passing by
appearing as if we are moving
100 miles an hour on a packed
bus of women & children

with my sunday's best on to spend
majority of the day heading north
patiently for 5 hours to spend 2 hours
with my estranged loved one
to share hugs, give kisses, take photos,
to try not to feel odd that this man
who i call father but rarely see him
& talk to him but he looks & feels familiar

those trips were never enough time
my father never stayed in one facility
long enough for me to get used
to the commutes & returning back south
to the city was always even weirder
in a packed bus full of women & children
crying, all the way down with me watching
the sun set in their eyes.

PURPLE FLOWERS

my sister's birthday is june 12th
she resembles my father in character
as i resemble my mother
so we don't always agree on things

when my father's health took
a wrong turn
we both agreed that
we would make arrangements
to prevent him from passing
on her birthday

i wanted her birthday to always be
a celebration for her life
that night we moved him to hospice
& they called us & explained
how medication was the only thing
keeping him alive,
so after midnight,
we stopped the medication

we knew it would only be
a matter of days
before he passes
the one piece of advice
i gave myself
through all of this
is i will never give a loved one morphine
that image will stay with me forever
no one & nothing prepares you for that

my father passed on june 13th
i was on my way to work
& received the phone call

everyone was either occupied
or not emotionally prepared
to identify the body

life & death has a lot
of paperwork attached to it

when i arrived everyone looked at me
as if they knew me, maybe because
i have my father's face

when i walked in
he was wrapped in white
the nurse told me he died peacefully
but i cant imagine any of this
was peaceful for him

he had purple flowers on his chest
i don't know want kind

i was the only member of my family
who saw him on his deathbed
i spoke to him once last time
laid on his chest & said good bye

when i left the hospital
i was a different person.

THE CLEAN OUT

the day after
my father's funeral
my mother said
"we have to clean out your father's apartment"

regardless of what
was going on
i couldn't let her do it alone

my father lived 10 minutes away from me
on jerome ave side of yankee stadium

we walked into his apartment
& it looked as it always has
the obligatory puerto rico plaques
the plates with painted beaches on them
the pictures of famous puerto ricans
& the two dozen flags in case he forgot
where he was from

he was in columbia presbyterian
for over a month so there were
many piles to rummage through

i started cleaning out his room,
a sea of papers & dusty books
full of secrets & chronicled moments

i didn't allow my mother in his room
because she has known him for fifty years
& loved him for forty-nine of them

everything could be a dagger
waiting to stab her

his room was hoarder like
with the amount of journals
magazines & books he had
in every corner

he told me he hid money in his room
& i found it in various places
typical lonely paranoid ex-con tactic

my mother asked me
"how did you find it?" i told her
"i'm his son, i'm borderline everything he is"

i reimbursed who needed
to be reimbursed
& took what needed to be taken

it was very quiet that day
in the apartment
only thing i heard
was dust swirling off the fan
not much conversation
no music

& usually when i visited him
the radio would be
playing a song he loved

but today was
a very quiet day.

CANDLES BY THE ALTAR

on my father's birthday
my mother lights a candle
with the images of guadalupe
i don't know why
puerto ricans don't
celebrate her by that name
the virgin mary is in most homes
when i visit overly religious
grandparents & mothers
we were never that way
a set of palms
an easter visit
& maybe a picture
of jesus somewhere
but we weren't that religious

after my uncle died
my mother started
in remembrance

but now she lights two
standing in front of
a picture of jesus
buddha & a cup of water
for los espíritus

& i don't know why
my mother is not a buddhist,
or a follower of santería
she's barely a catholic but
she believes that if

she gives respect to as many
of them as possible, they will
be taken care of

we light candles
by the altar
every so often now.

MEDICATED SLAVE

at fifteen
my father
told me he was
hiv positive
the memory
is burned
in my psyche

this man
who i am
hesitant to
call father
jail bird
dead beat
south bronx
puerto rican
junkie nights
old boyfriend
new roles
bad news
crumbling facade
statistical percentage

when he told me
he broke down
& cried for
obvious reasons
his thinking was
attached to his death

but to me i was still

on teenage angst full of
single mother raised venom

in the next 10 years
i saw him transition from
schedule obsessed ex con
to medicated slave
to everything revolved
around what time
he needed to take his meds
my father was not
academically educated
but his street smarts
& common sense was high
read everything twice
but it was always hard for us
to be spontaneous with
his interruptions of

"i have to go home, i have to take my meds"

he lived longer than most of his friends
but at the end he was a shell of himself

the young ox
the gym rat
the weekend athlete
the orchard beach tshirt model

he knew how to take care of himself
but i wish he would of started earlier
his life would of been very different
we would of been different.

LEFTY

my father was
left handed
his nickname
was lefty
but only took
left turns
while driving

in his life
he always
ended up
exactly right
where he
shouldn't be
where the
wicked &
the cursed
meet, if he
would of at
least made
one left turn
instead
of a right
then maybe
more rights
would have
happened
in his life
& then he
would have
not left

his hopes
& dreams
on the curb
waiting for
the next bus
that would
never arrive.

ONE YEAR LATER

its been a year since your passing
not much has changed &
yet everything has changed

i avoid my reflection
fearing to see you in the
darkness under my eyes

my mother & i speak about you often
we even had breakfast
at the diner you liked
i never eat breakfast
but i know you did

i spoke to sister about you
briefly but she's not as open
with me as she used to be
but i can't recall when she ever was
you passing the day after
her birthday was not easy

i learned the flamingos' song
"i only have eyes for you"
on guitar because i know
you enjoyed it

my mother walked in on me
practicing it, she looked at me & smile
i try not to remind her of you
even though we carry the same face

i lost my uncle as a teenager & my mother
& share an occasional cry in his honor
we will honor you also

thank you
for our last conversation
for allowing me to sit next to you
for answering the questions i had about fear

i spoke to my son the day after
he wished his condolences
sounded sad he wasn't with me

i was always amazed & in awe
how you two interacted
played like grandfather & grandchild
you & i never interacted like that
i'm glad my son shares no animosity
that i carried from my childhood

its been a year since by 10:00 am
i was speaking to you
on your deathbed
i poured the sorrow
that was built up from
the last 30 years
& i apologized for things
i can't remember

i wondered what part of me was upset
is it the child who was raised with no father?
or the teenager who had a father but rejected
him? or is it my own long distance

relationship with my son?

yes

when i hear doo wop
i hear your body move
when i see the yankees win
i feel your happiness

rest old man
you had a hard life
with great moments
reflect on those

my mother told me
that when i was born
she wanted to name me
after you & my grandfather

he said:

"no, miguel's in this family have had
hard lives, i don't want that for him,
lets name him..."

JUST AS THE DAY
WAS DAWNING

THE BLIND
STAGGERING DRUNK

be bold enough
to step outside in a morning
full of gin, it's something
everyone should try once

see how the world tilts to the left
how your feet sink into the concrete
grab the rainbows in the sky
put them in your pocket

watch how politics & religion all
look the same, just like church & state
they all look at you like vermin
even though you are still human

the material things in the world
lose all its importance
the only thing you care for is
a free seat, new socks, a good meal
& maybe a hello

food, clothes, shelter
& compassion
are the only things
most of us need
but in the hooplah of it all
we get lost in our closets
trying to hide our skeletons
dress them up in cotton

& cashmere never realize
that the closet is dark

no one sees them until
the door is opened
next time you look
at your reflection
tilt your head to the left
see how different
you, your world & your
priorities change

be bold enough
to be strong

be bold enough
to be weak.

SKETCHES FOR MY
EX-SWEETHEARTS

this is
the last poem about you
that will smell like your skin
to contain your fingerprints
where your hair is tangled in the words
that your voice in pressed in the paper
concerning the conditions of our hearts
with a reference of your curvature
in respect to your gentleness
relating to the colors of your kiss
with any relevance to your relevance
referring to the experience of your love
in the subject of your physical matter
or about our 12 month, 24 month, 36 month,
48 month affair

this is
the first where i am happy
that i no longer obsess over
your presence in my space
even after the fire
i destroyed the whole building
there is no intellectual property
left of our time together
it is found all over new york city
underwater & sun burnt

this is
the first sentence

i am taking back for myself
taking back so i can show
myself this is right

the first syllable
where i can enjoy the name
that you carry that used
to be a death sentence

this the first time
i can leave everything all behind
& not worry about it because
i am carrying myself for once

this is for me
not for muses
fairies & witches

this is for me.

THE GAMBLING
HIGHWAY

i've been told
the highway is for gamblers
which is why i walk the roads
that dead men have built with patience

i leave my mark
on corners where
saints have been murdered
its hard to be one in this city

in every other neighborhood
i change my face to reflect
the time of day
the purpose of the moment

in every other street
i carry a different name
in my mouth to help me move safely

the jesters & vagabonds
are showing me aces
as i walk by
they all have bullet holes in them
it must of saved their lives at least once

they all have skin like suede
tongues like whips
hands like granite
& hugs like stick ups

i've been taught to walk
with straight eyes & crooked feet
been told that every city
is not designed for my exploration

the puzzles of these cities
are the same as washington heights
or hackney or the west village or the bijlmer
or oakland or any red light district
it is built all over each other

every boy on the corner looks familiar
with the same hope in their eyes
& struggle in their breath

this life don't come easy
& majority claims some of us
stop thinking after we turned teenaged
& hormones took over

the highway is a gamble
& that's where i want to go
to take risks, to take chances

i was not built
to be born here
live here & die here

i want to leave my nuyorican accent
over different latitudes
make love in different longitudes
find beautiful things in corners
i've never seen

the television will never replace
the hunger to cut my teeth
on different tasting bricks
the world is waiting for me
what am i waiting for?

i run down the sky paths
of my life hoping the clouds will part

i am waiting
for another obstacle
to overcome

i will not worry about
the meaningless things in my life
when they're ready for me
they'll come for me but

they will not destroy me

tell them to keep their boroughs
i want new continents to claim
new sunsets to eat
new oceans to baptize in
new love to bury
in the earth that will one day grow

& if & when they ever catch me
i'll smile & tell them

"tomorrow i'll start again."

WHEN IN PARIS

i take a bus to the last stop
hopefully i am familiar
with the neighborhood

i want to see what the residents
of this town see
i visit the local bakery
buy a cupcake from them

i introduce yourself to
complete strangers
give directions to french
residents in bad french
but since i know where
they're going i'll feel confident
with speaking my bad french

i don't take photos of every landmark
i can buy postcards for that, i show my
friends what the buildings look
like on the other side of town
the ones where people
wear the same face
my mother wears live

i search for a local caribbean place
ask for a dish i never eat
in the states so i won't compare it with
camaradas el barrio, el malecon
or any other puerto rican/dominican eatery

i enjoy drinking water because the soda
taste different because of the sugar

i walk everywhere even in bad weather
go to the river seine & give thanks
to camus, celan & desnos

i go to louvre just to say i did
the mona lisa will be exciting for a
two minutes then i'll feel cheated

i visit notre dame & recite every quasimodo
reference you can think of, i admire the
craftsmanship of the old world

i hang out with mike ladd, we talk about
nyc & what paris looked like when it was
being invaded, we think about the possibilities.
i push tourists a little harder to let them know
i'm there, mike gives me clarity & tells me
"remember they've been built on top of each
other"

smile at every woman i catch staring at
my hair, if my french was better i would
actually hold a conversation but the day is
too beautiful to stand around

i visit a popular shopping store
& see a hat one sale then purchase it
ironically, i told myself earlier
i should buy a hat while i'm here &
enjoy answering when someone asks

"where did you buy your hat?"
"oh in paris"
it'll feel nice to tell someone
where you brought something

i eat nutella crepes in
honor of rey robles
he loves nutella

i ask if anyone knows any puerto ricans
they all decline & ask if i am moroccan

i go to the highest point of paris
& see the parisian landscape
see the sky so beautifully black

i see an old lady fall, i am grateful
i was there at that moment to help her up
i say thank you in english
ask her if she's okay
it doesn't matter if
she doesn't understand me
she knows by the look in my eyes
i am trying to help her
maybe i look like her grandson
maybe i don't

but it doesn't matter
i am grateful i was there.

i was there.

THE INEVITABLE ANALYSIS OF STANDING IN FRONT OF THE MIRROR

i try to let love be the initiator
to everything i do
& keep myself out of
my own harmful ways

because i have suffered at my own hands
& even though today may
not seem like a new day
i try to rediscover myself
i try to learn to love myself
i try this everyday

i've stopped spreading myself out so thin
started keeping myself compact, safe,
keeping my wild & purpose in my palm,
i even let the world know that they are genius
& beautiful & i mean it

i unplug once in a while
i don't let television or the internet
be my only source of inspiration &
information, there's a whole world
out there waiting for me
i introduce myself to them constantly
i stand on the corner
look at the things
both beautiful & ugly

perfect & flawed
take it all in & breathe deeply

when i see my reflection
i try to recognize myself in my older skin?

today i reminded myself that this is what i
walked myself to, that this is where i am
supposed to be at this exact moment
(standing in a bookstore in-between
non-fiction & fantasy)

i write on the subway walls

> *"dedicate yourself to your art*
> *& your art will dedicate itself to you"*

> *"respect your art*
> *& your art will respect you."*

funny enough if i get caught writing this
i'll be arrested for my art.

i have never wanted to be king of anything
kings get beheaded, even less is a gangster
i never wanted to be a gangster, they often
get killed too young

i like the concept of being an old man writer
who writes forever, until he forgets how's to

i've allowed myself to enjoy my faults
then remind myself i have work to do

i've learned how to be for simple reasons
cultivated the quiet of my body

i've shared something deeper than
myself with whom you choose like
music, laughter & pizza

in my insecurity i have a hard time trusting
in my foundation so i revisit
the original tools i started with

i've learned there will be
truth in my sadness
sadness in my logic
logic in my erratic
erratic in my happiness
happiness in my truth

i've learned to slow down
& love the moment
what happens after usually is amazing

i tell myself i'm handsome
in the morning, in the mirror
in the evening, naked, after a shower

i believe my words
even when i don't want to
unconditional love can
be a transformational experience
especially when it comes from yourself.

JUST AS THE DAY WAS DAWNING

stand in the spot
where the sun stands
the warmest natural
spot you could find

then sit down
& let everything go
forgive people who have
been evil towards you

who have tried to crumble your spine
with rumors of your worthlessness
do not believe them
they know nothing of you

they do not know how
your body levitates when you sleep
they do not know how
the wind takes turns learning
how to spin from you

forgive yourself
for the absent minded
moments of compassionless

we are flawed machines
we are allowed to fail
& in our failure is where we grow
& where we learn

forgive your past
for it is filled with
wrong decisions &
wrong men & wrong women
with hateful interludes
when your life was still
too new for you or anyone else
to understand it properly

forgive your present
for the immaturity
we still carry at times

where we forget we are grown
but not grown, it is all based

on perspective, if we never experience
new things how are we to grow

our age means nothing
in an age of monotony

we use it to track things like
progress, process & product

we are perfect organisms
of flesh & blood & water

see how the sun & heat
feel on our skin

see how it works in unison
we are interconnected

the sky is not for you
the sky is with you

the ocean is not for you
the ocean is with you

the animals are not for you
the animals are with you

the food is not for you
the food is with you

know your place
know your purpose

do not accept imperialism
as a way of life

do not accept capitalism
as a way of life

do not accept hate
as a way of life

do not accept love
as a way of life

find your balance
in everything you do

some will work correctly
& some will fail horribly
but understand each process

know your place in your skin
then your skin in the environment
then the environment in the world
then the world in the universe then
the universe in the universe in the universe

see how wonderfully small & large
we are at the same time

      let the beauty of everything
     be your beauty of everything
     be the beauty of everything

THANK YOU'S

to my father: lefty. rest in peace. i love you.
to my mother: the little lady. i love you.
to my sister. the rock. i love you.
to my son: you are the best boy ever! i love you!

to my extended family: angel zenon, vincent ramirez,
fifi perez, emmanuel mendoza,wilfredo maysonet,
glendaliz, hope, my TCK fam, vaz avedian, fernando
reals, charlie doves, angelo baque, bzar, antonio kels,
sege, smirk, chris maestro, dennis kim, mush, joe vega,
dave mendez, shaggy flores, carmen valentin, yanko
valentin, angel rodriguez, michael cirelli, mahogany l.
browne, luivette resto, gabriel ramirez, tyrek, cliff,
joseph perez, ish islam, reynold martin, mikal, kahlil,
samra & eli jacobs-fantauzzi, jeff chang, ying-sun,
sake1, baba israel, irfan rainy, wonway posibul, lemon,
suheir hammad, tony medina, willie perdomo, ekere
tallie, junot diaz, mike ladd, saul williams, aracelis
girmay, kumasi j. barnett, jason reynolds, rich villar,
wilkins frias, eduardo de leon, fish, dan sullivan, tim
stafford, jay lee, shihan, kelvin uffre, chris carambot,
jean shepherd, alex guzman, richard shepherd, walter r.,
orlando & camaradas, urban word nyc, nuyorican poets
cafe, voz alta, mental graffiti, youth speaks, papo &
george, capicu poetry, jose morales, apt78, jessica fagin,
chimene suleyman, adrian viajero roman, fresthetic,
mikey 1soul, randy q, ben rojas, adia & beans, andy
gonzalez, rudy m., cesar madura, d.katz, neil morgan,
justin zafran, wayne collins, my rojas family, my nazario
family, my joy family, all the venues & schools that
booked me, thank you.

& to amiri baraka & louis reyes rivera : rest in peace

BIOGRAPHY

bonafide rojas is a poet & has two previous collections
of poetry: *when the city sleeps (grand concourse press, 2012)
& pelo bueno: a day in the life of a nuyorican poet (dark souls
press, 2004).*

he currently lives in the bronx, new york. he started
grand concourse press to publish books whenever he felt he
should. you can find him riding the train playing air
guitar. he loves pizza, has a bad diet soda habit, collects
everything from comic books to guitars to blazers to
old photographs of his family.

he loves music so much he created a band called
the mona passage that performs once in a while. he's
grateful to be apart of the continuum of nyc poetry.

in his spare time he plays air guitar to everything.

thank you.
thank you.
thank you.

www.ingramcontent.com/pod-product-compliance
Lightning Source LLC
La Vergne TN
LVHW051558080426
835510LV00020B/3032

* 9 780615 908175 *